Clinical Trials Programming Using SAS 9 (A00-281) Exam Practice Questions & Dumps

Exam Practice Questions for SAS A00-281
LATEST VERSION

Presented By: Quantic Books

About Quantic Books:

Quantic Books is a publishing house based in Princeton, New Jersey, USA. , a platform that is accessible online as well as locally, which gives power to educational content, erudite collection, poetry & many other book genres. We make it easy for writers & authors to get their books designed, published, promoted, and sell professionally on worldwide scale with eBook + Print distribution. Quantic Books is now distributing books worldwide.

Note: Find answers of the questions at the last of the book.

QUESTION 1

Given the following data set:

subjid	trt	result	dtime	age
1		CR	0	56
2	A	PD	1	52
3	B	PR	1	47
4	B	CR	2	29
5	1	SD	1	39
6	C	SD	3	21
7	C	PD	2	90
1	A	CR	0	43
3	B	PD	1	56

The following output was generated from PROC PRINT.

Obs	subjid	trt	result	dtime	age
1	1		CR	0	56
2	2	A	PD	1	52
3	3	B	PR	1	47
4	4	B	CR	2	29
5	5	1	SD	1	39
6	6	C	SD	3	21
7	7	C	PD	2	90

Which program was used to prepare the data for this PROC PRINT output?

A. proc sort data=one out=two; by subjid;
run;

B. proc sort data=one out=two nodupkey; by subjid;
run;

C. proc sort data=one out=two nodup; by subjid;
run;

D. proc sort data=one out=two nodupkey; by subjid trt;
run;

QUESTION 2

This question will ask you to provide a line of missing code.

The following SAS program is submitted:

```
proc freq data=dist;
    <insert code here>
run;
```

to create the following output:

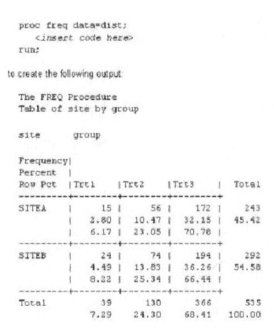

```
The FREQ Procedure
Table of site by group

site        group

Frequency|
Percent  |
Row Pct  |Trt1     |Trt2     |Trt3     |   Total
---------+---------+---------+---------+
SITEA    |    15 |     56 |    172 |    243
         |  2.80 |  10.47 |  32.15 |  45.42
         |  6.17 |  23.05 |  70.78 |
---------+---------+---------+---------+
SITEB    |    24 |     74 |    194 |    292
         |  4.49 |  13.83 |  36.26 |  54.58
         |  8.22 |  25.34 |  66.44 |
---------+---------+---------+---------+
Total         39      130      366      535
            7.29    24.30    68.41   100.00
```

Which statement is required to produce this output?

A.   TABLES site*group /nocol;
B.   TABLES site*group /norow;
C.   TABLES site*group;
D.   TABLES site*group /nocol norow;

QUESTION 3

Which statement correctly adds a label to the data set?

A.   DATA two Label="Subjects having duplicate observations"; set one;
run;

B.   DATA two;
Label="Subjects having duplicate observations"; set one;
run;

C.   DATA two;
set one;
Label dataset="Subjects having duplicate observations";
run;

D.   DATA two(Label="Subjects having duplicate observations"); set one;
run;

QUESTION 4

The following SAS program is submitted:

```
proc univariate data=WORK.STUDY;
    by VISIT;
    class REGION TREAT;
    var HBA1C GLUCOSE;
run;
```

You want to store all calculated means and standard deviations in one SAS data set. Which statement must be added to the program?

A.   output mean std;

B.   ods output mean=m1 m2 std=s1 s2;

C.   output out=WORK.RESULTS mean=m1 m2 std=s1 s2;

D.   ods output out=WORK.RESULTS mean=m1 m2 std=s1 s2;

QUESTION 5

Which program will report all created output objects in the log?

A. proc ttest data=WORK.DATA1 ods=trace; class
TREAT;
var RESULTS;
run;

B. ods trace on;
proc ttest data=WORK.DATA1; class TREAT;
var RESULTS;
run;

C. ods trace=log;
proc ttest data=WORK.DATA1; class TREAT;

var RESULTS;
run;

D. ods trace log;
proc ttest data=WORK.DATA1; class TREAT;
var RESULTS;
run;

QUESTION 6

Review the following procedure format:

```
PROC TTEST data=data;
    class group-variable;
    var variable;
run;
```

What is the required type of data for the variable in this procedure?

A. Character
B. Continuous
C. Categorical
D. Treatment

QUESTION 7

You want 90% confidence limits for a binomial proportion from a one-way table with PROC FREQ. Which option must you add to the TABLES statement?

A. BINOMIAL
B. BINOMIAL ALPHA=0.9
C. BINOMIAL ALPHA=90
D. BINOMIAL ALPHA=0.1

QUESTION 8

The following SAS program is submitted.

```
data ae;
   input PTNO AESOC $ 6-32 AEPT $ 34-56 ONTREAT $;
   cards;
2001 Cardiac disorders          Cardiac arrest          Y
2002 Infections and infestations Empyema                Y
2002 Hepatobiliary disorders    Hepatic failure         Y
2002 Infections and infestations Leptospirosis          Y
2003 Nervous system disorders   Cerebral hemorrhage     N
2004 Cardiac disorders          Cardiac arrest          Y
2004 Cardiac disorders          Atrial fibrillation     N
2006 Infections and infestations Wound infection        Y
2007 Renal and urinary disorders Renal failure          Y
2007 Gastrointestinal disorders Pancreatitis acute      Y
2007 Gastrointestinal disorders Gastric ulcer           Y
2008 Vascular disorders         Hypotension             Y
2008 Infections and infestations Sepsis                 Y
2010 Cardiac disorders          Cardiac arrest          Y
2010 Renal and urinary disorders Renal failure acute    Y
2011 Social circumstances       Homicide                N
;
run;

proc freq data=WORK.AE noprint;
   where ontreat="Y"; tables aesoc / out=WORK.FREQ1;
run;

proc print data=WORK.FREQ1 noobs;
   where aesoc="Cardiac disorders";
   var count;
run;
```

What result is displayed for the variable COUNT?

A. 1
B. 2
C. 3
D. 4

QUESTION 9

Given the following output from the TTEST Procedure:
Variable:

Variable: fastgluc

N	Mean	Std Dev	Std Err	Minimum	Maximum
6	7.6517	0.4999	0.2041	6.9500	8.3700

Mean	95% CL Mean		Std Dev	95% CL Std Dev	
7.6517	7.1270	8.1763	0.4999	0.3121	1.2262

DF	t Value	Pr > |t|
5	37.49	<.0001

What is the t-test p-value?

A. 0.3121
B. <.0001
C. 37.49
D. 0.2041

QUESTION 10

This question will ask you to provide a line of missing code.

Given the following log entry:

```
45        data adsl ;
46            merge dm    (in=indm)
47                disp (in=indisp);
48            by subjid ;
49            <insert code here>
50        run ;

MERGE ISSUE: subjid=003 indm=1 indisp=0
MERGE ISSUE: subjid=005 indm=0 indisp=1
NOTE: There were 4 observations read from the data set WORK.DM.
NOTE: There were 4 observations read from the data set WORK.DISP.
NOTE: The data set WORK.ADSL has 5 observations and 3 variables.
NOTE: DATA statement used (Total process time):
      real time          0.07 seconds
      cpu time           0.01 seconds
```

Which line of code would produce the blue notes in the log?

A. if indm ne indisp then output 'MERGE ISSUE: ' subjid indm indisp ;

B. if indm ne indisp then put 'MERGE ISSUE: ' subjid= indm= indisp=;

C. %if indm ne indisp %then %put 'MERGE ISSUE: ' subjid= indm= indisp=;

D. if indm ne indisp then put 'MERGE ISSUE: ' _all_ ;

QUESTION 11

Given the following log entry:

```
47          data hrates ;
48             merge dm hr ;
49             by subjid ;
50          run ;

INFO: The variable sexcd on data set WORK.DM will be overwritten by data set WORK.HR.
NOTE: There were 4 observations read from the data set WORK.DM.
NOTE: There were 4 observations read from the data set WORK.HR.
NOTE: The data set WORK.HRATES has 4 observations and 4 variables.
NOTE: DATA statement used (Total process time):
      real time        0.06 seconds
      cpu time         0.01 seconds
```

Which SAS system option adds the blue highlighted lines to the log?

A. INFO
B. MSGLEVEL=I
C. INVALIDDATA='I'
D. NOTES

QUESTION 12

A SAS report procedure results in the log below.

```
13          proc report data=vitals ;
14             column patid visit height weight sysbp diabp ;
15          run ;

NOTE: Multiple concurrent threads will be used to summarize data.
NOTE: There were 26 observations read from the data set WORK.VITALS.
NOTE: At least one W.D format was too small for the number to be printed. The
    decimal may be shifted by the "BEST" format.
NOTE: The PROCEDURE REPORT printed page 1.
NOTE: PROCEDURE REPORT used (Total process time):
    real time          0.01 seconds
    cpu time           0.01 seconds
```

What should you add to the PROC REPORT to address the blue note in this log?

A. Use DEFINE statements with the WIDTH= option set large enough to print all values for each variable

B. Specify COLWIDTH= option with a value large enough to print all values in the data

C. Use DEFINE statements where FLOW is specified for each numeric variable

D. Use a FORMAT statement with formats large enough to print all values for each numeric variable

QUESTION 13

Which validation technique involves two programmers writing separate programs to produce the same output, then comparing the result?

A. Independent Programming
B. Peer Matching
C. Identical Programming
D. Peer Review

QUESTION 14

A SAS program is submitted and the following log is written.

```
893 data WORK.CHECKVISITS;
894   set WORK.VISITS(keep=PATID VISDT0 VISDT1 VISDT2 VISDT3 VISDT4);
895   array VISDT(1:4);
896   do i=1 to 4;
897     if VISDT(i) ?VISDT(i-1) gt 10 then output;
898   end;
899 run;

ERROR: Array subscript out of range at line 897 column 21.
```

What is the cause of this error message?

A.   The ARRAY declaration is syntactically incorrect.

B.   The IF statement is syntactically incorrect.

C.   The DO loop tries to get a value from a variable which does not exist.

D.   The IF statement tries to get ARRAY elements which are not declared.

QUESTION 15

The following SAS program is submitted:

```
data WORK.TEST;
  set WORK.WGTCODE;
  if Subjcode='Wgt2' then Description='Over';
  else Description='Unknown';
run;
```

If the value for the variable Subjcode is "WGT2", what is the value of the variable Description?

A.   missing character value

B.   Unknown

C.   Over

D.   Wgt2

QUESTION 16

Given two data sets with the following variables:

Data Set HR Variables:
- SUBJID
- VISIT
- HRATE

Data Set DISP Variables:
- SUBJID
- VISIT
- STATUS

Each data set was sorted by the subject identifier (SUBJID) and merged together. The resulting log is shown below.

```
50        data hrates ;
51            merge hr disp ;
52            by subjid ;
53        run ;
```

```
NOTE: MERGE statement has more than one data set with repeats of BY values.
NOTE: There were 13 observations read from the data set WORK.HR.
NOTE: There were 6 observations read from the data set WORK.DISP.
NOTE: The data set WORK.HRATES has 13 observations and 5 variables.
```

Why is the blue note showing in the log?

A.   The variable VISIT occurs in both data sets but is not included in the BY statement.

B.   There are no observations with matching values for SUBJID in either data set.

C.   There are multiple observations with the same value for SUBJID in both data sets.

D.   One of the two data sets has multiple observations with the same value for SUBJID.

QUESTION 17

Given the following data set DEMOG:

SITE	PATID	DOB	SEXCD	RACECD	TRTMNT
1	1	11/25/1946	2	1	1
1	2	11/01/1972	1	1	2
1	3	10/13/1969	2	1	1
1	4	05/18/1958	2	1	2
1	10	05/24/1999	2	1	1
2	1	03/15/1974	1	2	1
2	2	01/04/1983	2	1	2
2	3	12/22/1963	1	1	1
2	4	12/28/1976	1	9	2
2	5	10/04/1958	1	1	1
2	10	07/05/1969	1	2	2

Which selection below would be considered hard-coding?

A. if sexcd eq 1 then sex = "Male" ;
else if sexcd eq 2 then sex = "Female" ;

B. if site eq 1 then sexcd = 2 ;
else if site eq 2 then sexcd = 1 ;

C. if site eq 1 and sexcd ne 2 then check = 1 ;
else if site eq 2 and sexcd ne 1 then check = 2 ;

D. birthdt = input(dob, mmddyy10.) ;

QUESTION 18

The following SAS program is submitted:

```
data WORK.DATE_INFO;
    X='04jul2011'd;
    DayofMonth=day(x);
    MonthofYear=month(x);
    Year=year(x);
run;
```

Which types of variables are DayofMonth, MonthofYear, and Year?

A. DayofMonth, Year, and MonthofYear are character.
B. DayofMonth, Year, and MonthofYear are numeric.
C. DayofMonth and Year are numeric. MonthofYear is character
D. DayofMonth, Year, and MonthofYear are date values

QUESTION 19

Given the following data set (AE):

subject	firstdt	aeterm	aestdt	day
001	28NOV2009	NOSEBLEED	27NOV2009	-1
001	28NOV2009	HEADACHE	03DEC2009	6
001	28NOV2009	FRACTURE	08DEC2009	11
001	28NOV2009	VOMITING	15DEC2009	18
002	13JAN2010	COUGH	13JAN2010	1
002	13JAN2010	FEVER	19JAN2010	7
002	13JAN2010	MIGRAINE	23JAN2010	11
002	13JAN2010	DIZZINESS	03FEB2010	22

Data will be reported by onset week. Day 1 ?7 is Week 1, Day 8 ?14 is Week 2. Events beyond Day 14 are assigned Week 3 and will be reported as Follow-up events.

Which statements properly assign WEEK to each event?

A.   if day > 14 then week = 3 ; else if day > 7 then week = 2 ; else if day > 0 then week = 1 ;

B.   if day > 0 then week = 1 ; else if day > 7 then week = 2 ; else if day > 14 then week = 3 ;

C.   select ;
when (day > 0) week = 1 ; when (day > 7) week = 2 ;
otherwise week = 3 ;
end ;

D.   select ;
when (day > 14) week = 3 ; when (day > 7) week = 2 ;
otherwise week = 1 ;
end ;

QUESTION 20

Study day is defined as DCMDATE minus RFSTDTC +1

DCMDATE
- is character data in YYYYMMDD format
- contains partial date values

RFSTDTC
- is character data in date9 format
- contains missing values

Which statement will compute the study day correctly without producing notes for missing values in the log?

A. STUDYDAY=DCMDATE-RFSTDTC+1;

B. STUDYDAY=input(DCMDATE,yymmdd8.)-input(RFSTDTC,date9.)+1;

C. If RFSTDTC^='' and length(DCMDATE)=8 then STUDYDAY=input(DCMDATE,yymmdd8.)-input(RFSTDTC,date9.)+1;

D. If RFSTDTC^='' and length(DCMDATE)=8 then STUDYDAY=input(DCMDATE,date9.)-input(RFSTDTC,yymmdd8.)+1;

QUESTION 21

A Treatment-Emergent Adverse Event (TEAE) is commonly defined as any event that occurs on or after the date and time of:

A. informed consent

B. baseline assessment

C. study enrollment

D. first dose of study drug

QUESTION 22

SIMULATION

The following question will ask you to provide a line of

missing code. Given the following data set work.vs:

```
subjid  visit sbp
 A0156        1 146
 A0156        2   .
 A0156        3 152
 A0156        4   .
 A0156        5 143
```

The following SAS program is submitted to create a new
data set that carries forward the previous value of sbp when
the value is missing.

```
data work.vs1;
  <insert missing code here>
  set work.vs;
  if sbp NE . then old_sbp = sbp;
  else sbp = old_sbp;
run;
```

In the space below, enter the line of code that completes
the program (Case is ignored. Do not add leading or trailing
spaces to your answer.).

QUESTION 23

This question will ask you to provide a section of missing code. Given the input SAS data set LABRAW:

```
PTID  LABTEST  DATE_1      DATE_2       LAB_1  LAB_2
1001  ANC      12/20/2010  12/27/2010   2.16   2.34
1001  HCT      12/20/2010  12/27/2010   0.43   0.5
1002  ANC      12/18/2010  12/26/2010   2.2    2.3
1002  HCT      12/18/2010  12/26/2010   0.3    0.4
```

The following SAS program is submitted:

```
data lab_new (keep = ptid labtest visit date result);
   set labraw;
   array dat(2) date_1 date_2;
   array num(2) lab_1 lab_2;
   <insert code here>
run;
```

The following output SAS data set LAB_NEW is produced:

```
PTID  LABTEST  VISIT  DATE        RESULT
1001  ANC      1      12/20/2010  2.16
1001  ANC      2      12/27/2010  2.34
1001  HCT      1      12/20/2010  0.43
1001  HCT      2      12/27/2010  0.5
1002  ANC      1      12/18/2010  2.2
1002  ANC      2      12/26/2010  2.3
1002  HCT      1      12/18/2010  0.3
1002  HCT      2      12/26/2010  0.4
```

Which DO LOOP will create the output SAS data set WORK.LAB_NEW?

A. do i=1 to 2;
visit=i; date=dat{i}; result=num{i}; output;
end;
B. do i=1 to 2;
visit=i; date=dat{i}; result=num{i};

end; output;
C. do i=1 to 2;
do j=1 to 2; visit=i; date=dat{j}; result=num{j}; output;
end;
D. do i=1 to 2;
do j=1 to 2; visit=i; date=dat{j}; result=num{j};
end; output;
end;

QUESTION 24

Given the following SCORE data set:

subject	visitn	visit	score
001	0	Week 0	151
001	1	Week 2	150
001	2	Week 4	.
001	3	Week 6	155
001	4	Week 8	157
001	5	Week 10	.
001	6	Week 12	.
001	7	Followup	152

Based on the concept of Last Observation Carried Forward, what will be the value for SCORE for the Week 12

A. 157
B. 152
C. missing
D. 151

QUESTION 25

The following SAS program is submitted:

```
data WORK.DATE:
   day=1;
   do while(day LE 7);
      day + 1;
   end;
run;
```

What is the value of the variable day when the data step completes?

A. 1
B. 6
C. 7
D. 8

QUESTION 26

Given the following vital signs data:

USUBJID	VISITC	VISITN	HR
1	Pre-screen	0	86
1	Screening	1	91
1	Day 1	2	.
1	Week 1	3	68
1	Week 2	4	73
1	Week 4	5	96
2	Pre-screen	0	84
2	Screening	1	.
2	Day 1	2	73
2	Week 1	3	73
2	Week 2	4	52
2	Week 4	5	59

Baseline is defined as the last non-missing value prior to Day 1.

What is the value for the change from baseline for Week 1

for Subject 2? A. -23
B. 11
C. -11
D. 23

QUESTION 27

Given the following data set WORK.DM:

subject	ge	sex	race	cbp
001	24	M	WH	NA
002	53	F	BL	YES
003	36	F	AS	NO
004	62	M	BL	YES
005	25	F	WH	YES
006	80	F	HU	NA

Note: cbp = Child Bearing Potential

The following SAS program is submitted:

```
data _null_ ;
  set WORK.DM ;

  if sex = "M" and cbp ne "NA" then put "CHECK: " subject= sex= cbp= ;
  else if sex = "F" and cbp eq "NA" then put "CHECK: " subject= sex= cbp= ;

run ;
```

Which subjects will appear in the LOG file?

A. 001 and 004
B. 001 and 006
C. 003 and 004
D. 004 and 006

QUESTION 28

Which function would be used to determine the number of elements in an existing array?

A. dim ()
B. n ()
C. sum ()
D. count ()

QUESTION 29

SIMULATION

Given the following work data set containing Treatment-Emergent Adverse Events:

subject	aebodsys	aedecod	aesev
001	NERVOUS SYSTEM DISORDERS	DIZZINESS	1
001	NERVOUS SYSTEM DISORDERS	HEADACHE	2
001	NERVOUS SYSTEM DISORDERS	HEADACHE	3
001	NERVOUS SYSTEM DISORDERS	DIZZINESS	2
001	NERVOUS SYSTEM DISORDERS	LETHARGY	3
002	NERVOUS SYSTEM DISORDERS	DIZZINESS	1
002	NERVOUS SYSTEM DISORDERS	DIZZINESS	2
003	NERVOUS SYSTEM DISORDERS	HEADACHE	3
003	NERVOUS SYSTEM DISORDERS	HEADACHE	3
003	NERVOUS SYSTEM DISORDERS	LETHARGY	2
004	NERVOUS SYSTEM DISORDERS	LETHARGY	2

AESEV (Severity): 1 = Mild, 2 = Moderate, 3 = Severe

And a By Severity table:

	Subject n (%)
NERVOUS SYSTEM DISORDERS	
Mild	n (p)
Moderate	n (p)
Severe	x (p)

In the space below, enter the numeric value of x for "Severe" events under HEADACHE.

QUESTION 30

The following SAS program is submitted:

```
data WORK.DATE;
    X="01Jan1960"d;
run;
```

Which value does variable X contain?

A. the numeric value 0
B. the character value "01Jan1960"
C. the date value 01011960
D. the code contains a syntax error and does not execute.

QUESTION 31

This question will ask you to provide a line of missing code.

Given the dataset RAWBP that is sorted by SUBJECT TEST WEEK:

SUBJECT	WEEK	TEST	VALUE
101	0	DBP	160
101	1	DBP	140
101	2	DBP	130
101	3	DBP	120
101	0	SBP	90
101	1	SBP	87
101	2	SBP	85
101	3	SBP	80

The following SAS program is submitted:

```
data bp;
    set rawbp;
    by subject test week;
    retain baseline;
    if first.test then baseline = .;
    if week = 0 then baseline = value;
    else if week > 0 then  do;
        <insert code here>
    end;
run;
```

Which statement must be added to the program to calculate relative change in percent (percent change) from baseline?

A. pct_chg = ((baseline - value) /baseline)*100;
B. pct_chg = ((value - baseline) /baseline)*100;
C. pct_chg = ((baseline - value) /value)*100;
D. pct_chg = ((value - baseline) /value)*100;

QUESTION 32

Which statement correctly creates a SAS date variable from a character variable?

A.   sasdate = input(chardate,date9.);
B.   sasdate = 'chardate'd;
C.   sasdate = put(chardate,date9.);
D.   sasdate = date(chardate,date9.);

QUESTION 33

The following SAS program is submitted:

```
data WORK.DIGESTL;
array Observe(3) $ 8 ('appendicitis','diverticulosis','gastroenteritis');
run;
```

What is the value of the second variable in the data set WORK.DIGESTL?

A.   diverticulosis
B.   divertic
C.   a missing value
D.   No variables are created.

QUESTION 34

Given the SAS data set WORK.VS1:

Subject	_Name_	Visit1	Visit2	Visit3	Visit4	Visit5
101	SBP	160	150	.	130	120

The following SAS program is submitted:

```
data WORK.VS2;
  set WORK.VS1;
  Total=mean(of Visit:);
run;
```

Which value will be assigned to variable TOTAL?

A. missing
B. 112
C. 140
D. 560

QUESTION 35

Given the data set HE:

USUBJID	HETERM	HESEQ	HEDUR
201027	HOSPITALIZATION	1	50
201027	HOSPITALIZATION	2	.
201027	HOSPITALIZATION	3	10
201027	HOSPITALIZATION	4	5
211046	HOSPITALIZATION	1	9
211046	HOSPITALIZATION	2	.

The following SAS Program is submitted:

```
data hosp;
   retain hospdurd;
   set HE;
   by usubjid;
   if first.usubjid then hospdurd=0;
   hospdurd = hospdurd + hedur;
   if last.usubjid;
run;
```

What will the values be of variable HOSPDURD for the two subjects?

A. 5, missing
B. missing, missing
C. 65, 9
D. 50, 9

QUESTION 36

A Statistical Analysis Plan defines study day as the number of days between the visit date and the date of randomization plus one day.

The following SAS program is submitted using a macro from the project's library:

```
data VS_SD ;
    set VS ;
    label rdt = "Randomization Date" ;
    label vdt = "Visit Date" ;
    VSDY = %studyday(rdt,vdt) ;
run ;
```

How is the STUDYDAY macro defined?

A. %MACRO studyday(rand, visit); &vdt. ?&rdt. + 1
%MEND studyday ;

B. %MACRO studyday(rand=, visit=); &vdt. ?&rdt. + 1
%MEND studyday ;

C. %MACRO studyday(rand, visit); &visit. ?&rand. + 1
%MEND studyday ;

D. %MACRO studyday(visit=, rand=); &visit. ?&rand. + 1
%MEND studyday ;

QUESTION 37

Which clause allows macro variable creation on a select statement in PROC SQL?

A. INTO

B. SYMPUT

C. AS

D. %MACRO

QUESTION 38

This question will ask you to provide a missing option.

Given an existing work data set (DM), the following code is submitted:

```
options <insert option here> ;

%MACRO prt(dsn=, version=) ;
  %if &dsn. ^= DIARY %then %do ;
    proc print data = &dsn. ;
      title "Print of WORK.&dsn. data set" ;
      footnote "Version Date: &version." ;
    run ;
  %end ;
%MEND prt ;

%prt(dsn=DM, version=2009-12-08) ;
```

Which OPTION causes the following messages to appear in the LOG file?

```
<option name>(PRT):  Beginning execution.
<option name>(PRT): Parameter DSN has value DM
<option name>(PRT): Parameter VERSION has value 2009-12-08
<option name>(PRT): %IF condition &dsn. ^= DIARY is TRUE
<option name>(PRT): Ending execution.
```

A. MPRINT

B. SYMBOLGEN

C. MLOGIC

D. MRECALL

QUESTION 39

The following SAS program is submitted:

```
%let Av=age;
%macro LABD(Av=weight);
%let Av=gend; %mend;
%LABD(Av=height)
%put Av is &Av;
```

What will be written to the SAS log?

A. Av is weight
B. Av is gend
C. Av is height
D. Av is age

QUESTION 40

Which statement assigns the current date to the character variable CURRDT?

A. currdt="&sysdate.";
B. currdt="%sysdate.";
C. currdt="sysdate.";
D. currdt="#sysdate.";

QUESTION 41

A report that you are working on will require the following header lines:

```
Table 5.4

Adverse Events

By Body System, Preferred Term, and Greatest Severity
```

Which code adds the second line of the header "Adverse Events"?

A. header2 'Adverse Events';
B. header2 = 'Adverse Events';
C. title2 = 'Adverse Events';
D. title2 'Adverse Events';

QUESTION 42

This question will ask you to provide lines of missing code.

```
<insert code here>
proc print data=work.AE;
run;
<insert code here>
```

Which ODS statements, inserted respectively in the two locations indicated above, create a report stored in a PDF file?

A. ods pdf open='AE.pdf'; ods pdf close;
B. ods file open='AE.pdf' type=pdf; ods file close;
C. ods pdf file='AE.pdf'; ods pdf close;
D. ods file pdf='AE.pdf'; ods file close;

QUESTION 43

Given the following demographic dataset:

```
                    DEMO
subject   trt  age  gender   race       site
01002     A    28   MALE     BLACK      01
06003     B    18   MALE     HISPANIC   06
04001     B    24   FEMALE   CAUCASIAN  04
02003     A    14   FEMALE   CAUCASIAN  02
06005     A    20   MALE     BLACK      06
01004     B    13   MALE     CAUCASIAN  01
```

Which program will generate a report where observations will appear in order by SITE SUBJECT and display column headers for each variable defined in the column statement?

A. Proc Report ;
column site subject trt age gender race ; define site/'Site',
subject/'Subject', trt/'Treatment', age/'Age', gender/'Gender',
race/'Race' ;
run;

B. Proc Report ;
column site subject trt age gender race ; define site,
subject, trt, age, gender, race ; by site subject ;
title 'Site   Subject   Treatment   Age   Gender
Race' ; run;

C. Proc Report ;
column site subject trt age gender race ; define site/order
'Site' ;
define subject/order 'Subject' ; define trt/'Treatment' ;
define age/'Age' ;
define gender/'Gender' ; define race/'Race' ;
run;

D. Proc Report ;
column site subject trt age gender race ;

define site/order style(header)={'Site'} ;
define subject/order style(header)={'Subject'} ; define
trt/style(header)={'Treatment'} ;
define age/style(header)={'Age'} ;
define gender/style(header)={'Gender'} ; define
race/style(header)={'Race'} ;
run;

QUESTION 44

Which statement will produce report output that can be opened in Microsoft Word?

A. ods rtf file='report.rtf';
B. ods doc file='report.doc';
C. ods type='word' file='report.doc';
D. ods rtf='report.rtf';

QUESTION 45

This question will ask you to provide a line of missing code.

```
                    DEMO
subject  trt  age  gender   race        site
01002    A    28   MALE     BLACK       01
06003    B    18   MALE     HISPANIC    06
04001    B    24   FEMALE   CAUCASIAN   04
02003    A    14   FEMALE   CAUCASIAN   02
0600     A    20   MALE     BLACK       06
01004    B    13   MALE     CAUCASIAN   01
```

Which statement must be added to the following program to create a page break in the report after each RACE grouping?

```
proc report data=demo ;
  column race subject trt age gender ;
  define race / order 'Race' ;
  define subject / 'Subject' ;
  define trt / 'Treatment' ;
  define age / 'Age' format=3. ;
  define gender / 'Gender' ;
  <insert code here>
run ;
```

A. break page / race;
B. break race / page;
C. break after race / page;
D. break after race;

QUESTION 46

The VISIT data set is multiple records per subject, sorted by usubjid vistdtc vistm and contains the following variables:

#	Variable	Type	Len
3	VISITNUM	Char	3
1	VISTDTC	Char	19
2	VISTM	Char	5
4	usubjid	Num	8

The DEATH data set is one record per subject, sorted by usubjid vistdtc vistm and contains the following variables:

#	Variable	Type	Len
3	DHREFID	Char	5
4	DHTERM	Char	200
1	VISTDTC	Char	19
2	VISTM	Char	5
5	usubjid	Num	8

Which program will combine the DEATH and VISIT data sets by matching records?

A. data data_1;
merge death visit;
by usubjid vistdtc vistm; run;

B. data data_1;
merge death visit; run;

C. data data_1;
set death visit;
by usubjid vistdtc vistm; run;

D. data data_1;
merge death visit;
by usubjid vistm vistdtc; run;

QUESTION 47

Which name is a valid SAS V5 variable name?

A. _AESTDTC
B. AESTARTDTC
C. AE-STDTC
D. AE_START_DTC

QUESTION 48

You have been asked to import an Excel spreadsheet.
What will lead to substantial differences between the
original Excel spreadsheet and the resulting SAS data set?

A. the number of rows to be read from the Excel file
B. the number of columns to be read from the Excel file
C. multiple value types within a single column
D. multiple value types within a single row

QUESTION 49

The following SAS program is submitted:

```
data BASE_BP (drop=vstestcd);
   set VS (keep=usubjid vsstresn vstestcd);
   if vstestcd in('DIABP','SYSBP');
run;
```

Which alternative program creates an equivalent BASE_BP data set?

A. proc sort data=VS (keep=usubjid vsstresn vstestcd) out=BASE_BP (drop=vstestcd);
where vstestcd in('DIABP','SYSBP'); by usubjid;
run;

B. data BASE_BP;
set VS (keep=usubjid vsstresn); if vstestcd in('DIABP','SYSBP');
run;

C. proc sort data=VS (keep=usubjid vsstresn vstestcd) out=BASE_BP (drop=vstestcd);
by usubjid;
if vstestcd in('DIABP','SYSBP'); run;

D. data BASE_BP (keep=usubjid vsstresn vstestcd); set VS (drop=vstestcd);
if vstestcd in('DIABP','SYSBP'); run;

QUESTION 50

Given the following data set:

STYSID1A DATE_TIME	SYSBP	DIABP	RESP
0001_0001 19961216:09:26	120	80	20
0001_0001 19961223:08:18	110	75	15
0001_0001 19961230:09:12	115	77	18
0001_0001 19970106:09:01	107	70	12
0001_0001 19970110:08:43	112	73	15

Which type of clinical trials data is this?

A. Demographics
B. Laboratory
C. Medical History
D. Vital Signs

QUESTION 51

Define.xml is an XML-based submission of a clinical study's:

A. results
B. metadata
C. data
D. protocol

QUESTION 52

Which CDISC standard is concerned with the development of simplified case report forms?

A. Clinical Data Acquisition Standards Harmonization (CDASH)
B. Operational Data Model (ODM)
C. Study Data Tabulation Model (SDTM)
D. Trial Design Model (TDM)

QUESTION 53

Given the following data set:

```
STYSID1A COLLDTM          HBA1C      GLUC  SGOT    SGPT
0001 0001 19961216:09:26   5.1       125   32.2    29.1
0001 0001 19961223:08:18   6.1       136   34.1    30.1
0001 0001 19961230:09:12   8.1       225   31.8    29.5
0001 0001 19970106:09:01   6.7       158    .      29.7
0001 0001 19970110:08:43   6.6       150   30.5    30.2
```

Which type of clinical trials data is this?

A. Laboratory
B. Baseline
C. Medical History
D. Vital Signs

QUESTION 54

Where would you store a value collected on a case report form but not defined in an SDTM domain?

A. RELREC
B. DM
C. SUPPQUAL
D. SC

QUESTION 55

Which statement correctly describes an aspect of a Phase II clinical trial?

A. randomized controlled multicenter trials on large patient groups
B. designed to assess the pharmacovigilance, pharmacokinetics, and pharmacodynamics of a drug
C. in vitro and in vivo experiments using wide-ranging doses of the drug
D. designed to assess how well the drug works

Answers

1. Correct Answer: B
2. Correct Answer: A
3. Correct Answer: D
4. Correct Answer: C
5. Correct Answer: B
6. Correct Answer: B
7. Correct Answer: D
8. Correct Answer: C
9. Correct Answer: B
10. Correct Answer: B
11. Correct Answer: B
12. Correct Answer: D
13. Correct Answer: A
14. Correct Answer: D
15. Correct Answer: B
16. Correct Answer: C
17. Correct Answer: B
18. Correct Answer: B
19. Correct Answer: A
20. Correct Answer: C
21. Correct Answer: D
22. Correct Answer: RETAINOLD_SBP;,RETAINOLD_SBP;
23. Correct Answer: A
24. Correct Answer: A

25.	Correct Answer: D
26.	Correct Answer: C
27.	Correct Answer: D
28.	Correct Answer: A
29.	Correct Answer: 2
30.	Correct Answer: A
31.	Correct Answer: B
32.	Correct Answer: A
33.	Correct Answer: B
34.	Correct Answer: C
35.	Correct Answer: B
36.	Correct Answer: C
37.	Correct Answer: D
38.	Correct Answer: C
39.	Correct Answer: D
40.	Correct Answer: A
41.	Correct Answer: D
42.	Correct Answer: C
43.	Correct Answer: C
44.	Correct Answer: A
45.	Correct Answer: C
46.	Correct Answer: A
47.	Correct Answer: A
48.	Correct Answer: C
49.	Correct Answer: A
50.	Correct Answer: D
51.	Correct Answer: B
52.	Correct Answer: A
53.	Correct Answer: A
54.	Correct Answer: C

55. **Correct Answer: D**